BIG CATS

PUMAS

Don Middleton

The Rosen Publishing Group's
PowerKids Press™
New York

This book is dedicated to my wife Sue and my daughters Jody and Kim. Without their support, my writitng and other wildlife adventures would not have been possible. Also, a special thanks to author and friend Diana Star Helmer for believing in me.

Published in 1999 by The Rosen Publishing Group, Inc.
29 East 21st Street, New York, NY 10010

First Edition

Book Design: Danielle Primiceri

Photo Credits: Cover © 1996 PhotoDisc, Inc.; pp. 4, 6, 9, 13, 20, 22 © Gail Shumway/FPG International; pp. 11, 15 © Lee Kuhn/FPG International; p. 16 © Joseph Van Os/Image Bank; p. 19 © Dennis Hallinan/FPG International.

Middleton, Don.
    Pumas / by Don Middleton.
        p.   cm. — (Big cats)
    Includes index.
    Summary: Discusses the habitat, lifestyle, diet, physical characteristics, and future of the American big cats known as the puma, cougar, mountain lion, or panther.
    ISBN 0-8239-5211-8
    1. Pumas—Juvenile literature. [1. Pumas 2. Endangered species.] I. Title. II. Series.
QL737.C23M548 1998
599.75'24—dc21   97-49016
                                                                                    CIP
                                                                                     AC

Manufactured in the United States of America

CONTENTS

BIG CATS

Pumas are one of the eight **species** (SPEE-sheez) of "big cats." Pumas and jaguars are the only big cats that live in North, South, and Central America. But pumas are not called "great cats" like tigers, lions, jaguars, and leopards. That's because pumas cannot roar. Because pumas are not great cats, their young are called kittens, just like baby house cats.

Pumas are found all the way from Alaska in North America to the southern tip of South America. Pumas are also found in Florida.

Some scientists believe that over 50,000 pumas live in the wild. ▶

4

CATS IN THE AMERICAS

Even though pumas cannot roar, they do
make other sounds such as whistles, chirps,
and even loud screams.

6

In North America, pumas are sometimes called **cougars** (KOO-gerz) or mountain lions. There a nineteen **subspecies** (SUB-spee-sheez) of pumas subspecies that lives in Florida is called a Flori panther, even though it's really a puma.

Pumas are about 27 inches tall and can weigh 225 pounds. However, one large male puma Arizona weighed over 300 pounds! The body puma can be up to six feet long. Female pum usually smaller than males.

BUILT TO JUMP

Pumas have long, thick tails that can be two to three feet long. Their heads look small on their long bodies. Most pumas have gray or light brown fur. On some pumas, the fur may be a reddish color or almost black.

Of all the big cats, pumas are the best jumpers. Pumas have long legs with strong muscles. Because of their strong legs, pumas can leap over 40 feet across flat ground without putting their paws down. When they want to climb, pumas can jump straight up to branches or rocks that are fifteen feet above the ground.

◄ Pumas are so strong that they can jump twelve feet into a tree while carrying a deer in their mouths!

9

FANGS AND CLAWS

Pumas are **predators** (PRED-uh-terz). Their most common **prey** (PRAY) is deer. In North America, pumas hunt all kinds of deer, such as mule deer, blacktailed deer, and large elk. Pumas also hunt smaller animals, such as ground squirrels, beavers, and rabbits.

Pumas hunt by **stalking** (STAW-king) their prey. First, a puma moves slowly and quietly toward its prey. When it gets close enough, the puma will chase the animal and knock it to the ground. The puma's sharp claws help it hold the prey. Then pumas use their sharp front teeth, or fangs, to kill the animal by biting its throat.

A puma's fangs are actually called canines. ▶

THE ADAPTABLE CAT

Pumas can **adapt** (uh-DAPT) to almost any living area. They live in forests, swamps, tropical jungles, grasslands, desert-like areas, and mountain areas. Some pumas even live close to towns and cities. The only other big cats that live in so many different places are leopards. Except for mothers with kittens, pumas live alone.

Pumas will hunt for food both during the day and at night. However, when people live nearby, pumas will hunt only when it gets dark so people can't see them. Pumas climb trees or find places on the ground to hide in when they are resting or sleeping.

◄ After a puma kills its prey, it usually drags the animal back to a secret place deep in the forest to eat.

BABY PUMAS

Pumas can **mate** (MAYT) at any time of year. To **attract** (uh-TRAKT) a male puma, a female puma leaves a special smell on the ground. She also screams loudly to attract males. After mating, the male leaves. In three months, the female may give birth to one to three kittens.

When puma kittens are born, they are blind. They usually weigh just over one pound and are about twelve inches long. Puma kittens have large spots on their fur, and their tails have dark rings. The spots and rings begin to disappear when the kittens are six months old. By the time the kitten is one year old, the spots and rings are gone. The kittens drink their mother's milk to grow big and strong.

The spots on puma kittens' fur help the kittens hide in thick bushes. ▶

GROWING UP

Mother pumas always guard their young except when it is time to hunt. Before hunting, a mother puma hides her kittens in thick bushes or a **den** (DEN) to keep them safe. The kittens stay very still and quiet until she returns. When the kittens are about six weeks old, they start to hunt with their mother.

Puma kittens watch their mother closely as she hunts. She teaches them which animals are good to eat and how to catch them. She also teaches them how to stay safe.

◀ When they are two years old, puma kittens are ready to leave their mothers and live on their own.

PUMAS AND PEOPLE

Pumas hardly ever attack people. However, sometimes people hike in the forests or mountains where pumas live. If a person bothers or frightens a puma, that person is in danger of being attacked. Attacks can also happen when people build their houses where pumas live. The pumas do not move away. And when people and pumas live so close together, they can sometimes get in each other's way. Sometimes when the pumas get hungry, they hunt dogs or cats that live nearby.

Farmers and ranchers often get angry at pumas. The pumas attack and kill the ranchers' and farmers' cattle and horses. When this happens, the pumas may be shot.

Pumas that attack peoples' pets or farmers' animals don't know that they are doing something wrong. ▶

PUMAS IN ZOOS

Pumas live very secret lives. They usually stay hidden whenever people are nearby. This makes it very hard to see pumas in the wild. For most of us, a zoo is the only place where we can see pumas.

Zoos are helping to save the pumas known as Florida panthers. Because just a few of these animals are still alive, some have been caught and put in zoos. These pumas are mating and having strong, healthy kittens. In the future, some of these kittens or their young may be set free in wildlife parks in Florida.

◀ Pumas are very shy, even in zoos. They often run away when people come near. One of their favorite places to hide is high on a tree branch.

A FUTURE FOR PUMAS

Many pumas live in the wild. But steps must be taken now to protect these amazing animals. In many places in the Americas, the forests and grasslands are being turned into farms, roads, cities, and country homes. While these changes are important for people, we must make sure that we save enough room for pumas. Some countries are putting aside land for nature parks where pumas will be able to live safely. Other countries are doing very little.

We must learn that all animals need wild places where they can live free and safe.

GLOSSARY

adapt (uh-DAPT) To change because of new conditions.
attract (uh-TRAKT) To draw someone or something to you.
cougar (KOO-ger) Another name for a puma.
den (DEN) A small, usually hidden living area.
mate (MAYT) A special joining of a male and female body. After mating, the female may have a baby grow inside her body.
predator (PRED-uh-ter) An animal that kills other animals for food.
prey (PRAY) An animal that is eaten by another animal.
species (SPEE-sheez) A group of animals that are very much the same.
stalking (STAW-king) To sneak up on an animal while hunting.
subspecies (SUB-spee-sheez) A group of animals that are very much the same but have small differences.

WEB SITES:

You can learn more about pumas at these Web sites:
http://www.primenet.com/~brendel/
http://home1.gte.net/marydiaz/animals/bigcats.htm

INDEX